I0182588

Terence Storm Publishing

Web: www.TerenceStormPublishing.com

This publication is designed as a parody and is meant for humorous purposes only.

TITLES BY T.J. RUSS:

Everything President Obama is Doing to Keep America Free, Strong, and Prosperous

Why Sarah Palin is the Most Dangerous Woman in America

The Audacity of Hype

Wanted: Why Rush Limbaugh, Glenn Beck, and Sean Hannity are the 3 Most Dangerous Men in America

The Obama Border Agency

INTRODUCTION:

Are You Offended by This Book?

We hope not! This book is intended to make you laugh... not get angry. It is a novelty product that utilizes the old fashioned comedy of parody. This is a style of comedy that goes back to the 16th century. The Random House Dictionary of the English Language says "Parody" is "a humorous or satirical imitation of a serious piece of literature or writing."

Parody has been used throughout history as a fun way to make social and political points. In today's world of dirty politics where people say and do all kinds of very negative and offensive things, we feel that this form of comedy is more appropriate.

So don't get angry that this book is blank. Have a good laugh. This is the intention of this book and hopefully the person who provided this book to you. We kept the price low, so even those who purchased it not realizing it was a parody book would not be upset.

Besides being a fun political statement, the blank pages inside this book can be used as a journal, sketch pad, address/phone book, diary, or any number of other ideas. Be creative!

Finally, if you love this book and want to order large quantities, contact the person you received this book from and ask about discounts or visit www.TerenceStormPublishing.com. Or, if you have the desire to publish your own parody book similar to this title, visit our website for information on how we can help you publish your own parody book at a very reasonable price.

www.ingramcontent.com/pod-product-compliance
Lightning Source LLC
Chambersburg PA
CBHW032133040426
42449CB00005B/216
* 9 7 8 1 9 3 3 3 5 6 8 8 4 *